Mechanics Of A Nigga

By Timothy Hollins

Contents

Preface

The African American race has been systemically conditioned to the degrading, and unjust social propaganda, teachings, preaching, and ideologies established by and for the benefit of the 'elite'. We, as African Americans, have been manumitted from chattel slavery since the late 1800's, but have fallen victim to countless injustices and practices before and after this so-called emancipation by a society we were forced to coexist in. However, in the early 1800's, a number of White Americans sought out to colonize us from their race. Of course, this came after they had entrapped, stolen, and enslaved us as a people, and rendered us upon western shores they violently took from the indigenous Natives, a land they named America…their land of the free.

After the enslavement of countless Africans, White American aristocrats, along with their 'common' fellowman, deemed it a problem to equate people of African decent with the freedom and equal rights they had shed blood for in their American Revolution. They devised many legislative polices, programs, groups, assemblies, theories, sciences, ideologies, etc., to support their racist mentalities towards the African American race, which were implemented on a national level and still exist today. The more liberal and radical Whites believed African Americans should be free and desegregated in America's society, but their thinking also placed them, White Americans, as the superior race. With all the harsh and tainted methods they introduced, practiced, and repeatedly ascribed to us, the African American, as uniform to our very nature and identity, many of us has subconsciously subscribed to and taken on these negative depictions and ways.

We, as African Americans, demonstrated and projected idea temperament, ethics, dignity, courage, spirituality, and love during our many years of struggle, and every activist during those years, whether documented in America's history or unrecorded and unrecognized, were indeed heroes. This is a history we should have reverence towards. This is a people worth celebrating, but many of us have forgotten our parents, grandparents, and ancestors' struggle. And in doing so, their legacy (our present and future) has been dishonored.

Those who serve this injustice to such a great race of people commit an even more horrific crime by not passing on our people's bravery and heroics throughout history to their children, which in turn causes a multitude of the new generation to live in disconnect with their heritage and history *(Cause and effect)*. All they have learned or will know of their own race is what White America instills within them…the negative depictions. This lost and confused group of people that has succumb to White America's ideology and tearoom rhetoric of what they consider a 'sub-class', has taken on their very own identity… not in race, but in mind. And in this obscure and demented way of thinking lies today's '***nigga***'!

Acknowledgements

I would like to thank God first and foremost, for continuously blessing me with the opportunity to share my literature with so many, and for His daily watch and protective hedge over me. I definitely would like to thank my cousin, Anthony Staples, for so many long hours of conversations and the knowledge he has shared with me on every aspect of life. I would also like to acknowledge and thank my mother, sister, daughter, nieces, and nephew for their continued support of my dreams. And to the ones I consider genuine friends, thank you! Love you guys.

Timothy Hollins/LSohl

Racial Metonymy

Disclaimer: The ideals and definitions found in this paper are strictly of the opinion and perception of the writer formed from research, and a lifetime of observations, and interactions with 'said' people.

Mechanic: (usually used with a plural verb) routine or basic methods, procedures, techniques, or details: the mechanics of running an office; the mechanics of baseball. (Dictionary definition)

Nigga: (noun) an achromic individual of no particular ethic belonging, whose personal characteristics and attributes, single or often combined, are those of zombie comparison, conning, carefree, trifling, self-centered, having an amassing psyche, hateful, acute jealousy, stupid, stubborn, low morals, amoral, little to no pains of consciousness, poor work ethics when pertaining to being productive, destructive, excuse hoarding, and negative in nature (author's definition)

The label, 'nigga', can be heard in colorful cadence from the mouths of individuals in every social caste no matter what level of hierarchy or echelon, and depending on the user, in different contexts. Some believe they use this label in a 'positive' manner (if there can truly be such) when referring to another person as a friend or having a family-like bond with that individual. Example: "That's my nigga!" Same as/equivalent to, "That's my homeboy/girl or friend", or "What up, nigga?" which can be translated and/or interpreted as, "What up bro/sis?" The label, by this defined usage, is still considered degrading, and is frowned upon by 'knowledgeable' society due to the word's origin and the traumatic history this label carries and embodies. This brings us to the second usage of the label by said society, which is disseminated and widely used in a demeaning manner and context, to relegate the person's worth and to describe that person's peculiar behaviors and negative disposition.

Niggas, portraying nothing short of stupidity in 'their' own foolish society, have been defined in a racist society by color, and linked to the ethnicity of the African American. And what's even sadder, we as a Black race, have embraced this 'bottled' and poisonous term as part of our culture, the same culture defined by hard work, intellect, nobility, pride, God-fearing, regal, and resilience to name but a few of our true attributes. This label dates back as far as the Atlantic or transatlantic chattel slave trade, and over time the label has been converted from Caucasian antebellum 'nigger' and 'niggrah' to present day African American 'nigga'. But when referencing this label, a closer look brings clarity to the way it is being used in the negative context which is actually describing and addressing the person's behavior rather than that person's ethnic belonging. This then, by definition, cannot be restricted to a race, social class, or sex any more than a person labeled a thief, killer, or fool. But all too often my people act as poster child and epithet to this brute negative. What I will discuss is the merging of 'nigga's' noun and adjective context by society in an attempt to expose the propensity of this modern day label and it's grim usage.

"…I walked the banks of Jordan to the great Mississippi; blistering and sore
only to encore what I dreamed even more than a tomorrow.
What I saw was you. What-I-saw… was you!!!
What I see is each of you
I-touch- your life with memories
You are my legacy
You are the scent of my blood and cries
and infinite pride I put in the winds…
You are 'Me'

"You Are Me"
LSohl

    We, the human race, are often deceived to and/or by the very society we inhabit. Often times we have what I consider a 'warped sense of reality' when pertaining to the many facets of 'accepted' behaviors, personal interactions, and people skills. Individuals functioning inside the limits of this 'warped sense of reality' tends to use a tilted moral scale in grave need of calibration, and a small distorted mirror reflecting their life…a life that's ghostly and nonexistent to the rest of the world. At times these individuals will revel and bathe in 'negative' behaviors due to both ignorance and stupidity, promoting and attempting to drum up support for their tainted actions and ideas with the hope that these actions and ideas wildfire throughout their surroundings. Why would anyone want to highlight such behaviors and ways of thinking? This answer varies with each individual that has allowed themselves to be boxed in the dark confines of such a mind state. Some seek acceptance and attention while others are simply lost, confused, or just feebleminded. They embrace the behaviors, interactions, and social skills 'normal' society deemed as unacceptable, and flaunt them in their everyday lives not only because they view these differently, but often times just to go against the grain and to be seen as subversive towards this established society they reside in.

    The persona created builds momentum when family, community, and society fails to redirect and restructure the individuals, now allowing that momentum to become a juggernaut of little to no mental and moral substance, a life of excuses, and a fool, which are all key components in the make-up of today's 'nigga'.

    Like every person, each member of the African American race has countless facets when referencing the peculiarities and idiosyncrasies of the individual. These many components differ in range from social, emotional, psychological, physical, etc., which in term defines the person's diversities. Some components of our behavioral make-up are learned and conditioned into our conscious minds; components that are somewhat of a controlled situation or circumstance, while others can be accredited and associated to the nature of each person. With said particular behavioral elements, the individual has little to no control as these behaviors are genetically encoded in each person. These elements are often times referred to as the 'nature' or propensity of each person.

    While some of us possess the loyal, honest, goodwill characteristics, to name but a few, that 'normal' society is accepting of, just as many in society reside on the opposite end of the character spectrum. Some of us surf freely in the corrupted waters of negativity, possessing unsettled/restless spirits with mean, ill-willed, and negative natures. Such attributes can often be ascribed to the 'nigga'! A 'nigga' loves drama. A 'nigga' lives for frivolous and inessential controversy, with an amoral mind-state; perpendicular and so unparalleled to a state of nirvana. These elements aren't necessarily learned behaviors, but are more of the person's natural propensity. Can such behaviors or traits be rehabbed or reconditioned to a more suitable and positive mind state? This depends solely of each individual. This requires self-reflection or looking at the person 'in the mirror'… something that is definitely easier said than done. Many of us struggle with this simple concept on a daily basis; starting with self and working on self to change the wrongs that we "can" see within ourselves.

"…In the damp and cold crevasses of the darkest mental caves
await me to duel with a future me; we duel till death.
Ridding myself of the wealth of an empty and mundane existence
So I'm lost…"

Scribbled Soliloquy
LSohl

But what if we can't see the negatives? What if we feel as though we aren't committing any wrongful deeds or negative actions with the behaviors and interactions displayed, and haven't the faintest clue as to the negatives others see in us? Sort of like tone deafness but referencing character and behavior. So how can one convince a person like this that his or her brain's 'way of thinking' when it comes to behaviors, the very thing that produces the thoughts is wrong? To convince the brain that it is wrong! This was a question my cousin posed to me once, and I haven't the faintest clue. The risk-takers in this profession have their jobs cut out for them in my opinion. But again, the nigga has an amoral take on things. It isn't that he/she can't differentiate the rights and wrongs, it's that he or she doesn't concern themselves with them. Their behaviors are on a conscious level to them, but the mental manufacturing of such behaviors are theoretically thought to be developed in a subconscious state, or genetically encoded; meaning these actions can't be met with any resistance from said person. The subconscious and conscious are said to be at constant ends with each other when thinking and carrying out the "next" move. This is but one explanation as to 'why' a nigga acts the way he/she does.

Some that fall in the 'underclass' of 'nigga' has full control of their actions, but readily employ these behaviors on society as though a peacock spreading its beautiful feathers. Some are experimental with the behaviors of this 'underclass' due to events in their personal life (bad intimate relationships or friendship turn sour, stresses, etc.), while some of these self-imposed experiments may be due to a trauma one has experienced or are experiencing (personal losses, the feeling of being victimized, etc.) that moves them into a mind-frame of F.T.W. (fuck the world), and they react in such a manner until they are met with forces that enlighten them; forces (spirituality, positive people and/or circumstances) that restores their previous mind-state. This only addresses the experimental niggas' mind-state! Those that live and revel their entire life or most of their life in the 'underclass' are surely not experimenting. These 'ways' are their ways.

My cousin always says to me, "Cuz, it's hard to get along with a nigga. You can't tell a nigga shit!" Excuse after excuse is what you get from a 'nigga'.

*****

 'Can't get in a bar fight if you don't go to the bar!': one of my favorite adages. If you sat at the far corner of a bar all alone, quiet and to yourself while sipping on whatever you had desired, and some meathead comes over and physically assaults you (obviously unprovoked), you now find yourself in the center of a brawl. But you did nothing wrong…right? You were minding your own business, and weren't pestering anyone. So, how did the altercation ignite? Who knows? Maybe the meathead was a nigga. But you share some of the blame still.

 You can still find fault in your actions. You put yourself in an environment that heightened the risk of a brawl…the bar! And even though the situation was unprovoked on your part, you were in the 'bar'. This is one way to reflect on the actions you took, and learn from those actions. But far too many of us make excuses for each and everything we do. These types of people can always seem to justify all of their actions. A nigga is the archetype to this particular mindset, exemplifying the likes of an illusion; excuse-hoarding individuals. Grand illusionists! They always find a way to justify the wrongs they impose on others, and in their lives. And in this justification, they are openly admitting to nothing because they feel as though they are not wrong.

 Prime example, how many of you can relate to that one person you have loaned money to; the nigga? When they come to you asking of the favor, they already have pre-established terms on their part as to when they will return the money. *"Can I borrow $20? I'll pay you back next Friday."* The next Friday arrives and several Fridays after that, but you never received that very small loan back, so of course the next encounter you have with the individual, naturally you asks about the money. To no surprise, they don't have it so they give you some explanation as to why. Maybe they had to pay whatever bill, or a family member got sick, or they got robbed or lost it on the way to pay you, or maybe it was the big story on your local news you never heard about of the cat being stuck in a tree and it would only come down for a special formulated milk from Greece that the cat desired. So he/she, being the kindhearted person they are, gave the owner, an elderly lady, the $20 to purchase the milk.

 All of this has not a thing to do with the terms the person, him/herself, set on paying back the money. Now, in this small and very common situation two things have come into existence when interacting with a nigga…first, the excuses of course, and secondly the 'victim' role. The borrower becomes the victim once you ask the whereabouts of the money you loaned. The borrower reaches out to every associate the two of you have in common and tells them of how petty you are for "hounding" him/her down for twenty measly dollars. *"Can you believe how he is acting over that little change? I mean damn, is he that broke to be hounding me down for twenty damn dollars?"* The borrower has now developed a negative attitude towards you with each encounter afterward. If, indeed, you ever do get the money back, the return will not be under the same pleasant and cordial interactions present when you loaned the money.

 What was initially a pseudo-feeling of appreciation and gratitude on the behalf of the nigga has been transformed to a feeling of compounded resentment and bitterness towards you. The borrower feels appalled and offended that you would even come at them asking for the $20 back. They have now painted you in their minds as a petty and simple person, and themselves as a victim. That's a nigga's mentality. He/she never sees the fact that it was a loan, and that you did them a 'favor' by making this loan. And that loan is like any other bill which needs to be paid back on the agreed upon terms and date set.

When my monthly electricity bill is due, I cannot go to my service provider and tell them that I had the money to pay my bill but a cat was stuck in a tree…and neither will the nigga try that excuse on their electricity provider. So why try to make excuses to the person they borrowed the money from because no matter who loaned it or how small the loan is, it's to be treated like any other bill they have acquired. But in their minds, somehow the personal loan is different and not as important. They can always shift the playing field in their favor, and they seek out people of like-minds to agree with their wrongs only to justify their actions. So by you asking for that loan back, you have also put another piece in play in this chain reaction of events that's putting you at fault; the attack on your character by the nigga. Either you are broke for wanting such a small amount of cash back, or you *"think you're more than the next man, anyways."* This is why the nigga goes around and tells his/her version of the episode. He/she feels as thought they have to beat you to the punch in telling their biased narrative, as if you would really exert your energy in doing so. And in doing this, they feel the need to paint the picture they want people to see you as which is the picture they have painted in their warped minds. So after much effort on their part to reach as many people as they can in order to tell them of how you 'are', the consensus among like-minded niggas is often times *"You always have thought you were more than others,"* and *"You think you're something."* We can all relate to this scenario; a situation I'm sure most have encountered.

Or maybe you was of the unfortunate to run into the deceitful, good-for-nothing nigga that needs the money from you to pay a bill, so they have to include the sympathy card by letting you know that it's (the loan) more so for the sake of their young kids…as if you can be held accountable in some way for the children's well-being. This card is readily flashed to play on your humanity. They will actually go so far as to ask you for your money to pay THEIR bills while at the same time cuffing (keeping and stashing) the money they already had in order to party and 'good-time' it away. So in actuality, you have financed their good time if you gave them your money. This, my friend, is a trifling nigga! These kind attempt to be very persuasive, but if you recognize and accept the character of this person, you would quickly come to your senses, and move on with your money still deep inside your pocket. So in these short and minute interactions with a nigga, several negatives in a chain reaction was put into play resulting from dealing with a nigga; the excuses, them as victims, your character being under attack, deceitfulness, and controversy; all because you tried to do someone a favor. ***"The road to hell is paved with good intentions!"***

The mindset of a nigga is either stagnant or progressive in nature; never at a decline when speaking on the negative behaviors and ways of thinking. He/she is a destructive individual when referring to their effects on a social and environmental level. To susceptible minds, they can cause havoc. The impressions they leave on a person aren't held in high regards, and if they are able to influence some, it's never an influence or effort to rally the individual in becoming an upstanding citizen. Often times they corrupt and suggest that the person take on their nigga ways.

In neighborhoods that houses niggas, they will tear up their homes, burglarize working people's homes, steal anything not bolted down and some things that are, destroy and vandalize property, be loud and obnoxious; all resulting in bringing down the value of that neighborhood. So in society's ecosystem, what worthiness does a nigga hold; what is their role? Again, I say destruction! They are 'shapeless', never possessing a productive or standup characteristic. They lie continuously. They are deceitful, freeloading, and trifling. They always seem to exert too much energy in an effort to "get over" on people or society with their watered-down manipulating efforts. They destroy lives and families if they are allowed in. They destroy positive ways of thinking if they are allowed in. They destroy institutions, parks, public buildings and structures, events, communities, etc., if they are allowed in. The nigga, in this regard, takes on the "American way" by destroying wherever they go. This is what America was built on; destruction. The founding fathers, or tyrants if rightly labeled, were of a destructive nature. They killed off the native dwellers of what was post-labeled America either through exposing them to their sicknesses, or though violence. So in retrospect, can the Caucasian race rightfully point a finger at any group of people and label them destructors? And can this destructive nature the nigga possess, be linked to the conditioning society has placed upon them since the start of this country, or maybe it's just the nature of humans in general that is destructive?

We can all point fingers and bold the wrongs and problems of the world, but how many of us actually try to change things for the better? I pose this question to anyone in all areas and aspects of life with the exception of the nigga because a nigga is hardheaded. "*You can't tell a nigga shit!*" Most will probably associate the nigga to the uneducated black race, but again, if we are addressing the nigga as defined in actions, it is not limited to a race, educational background, or social class. You have 'educated niggas' also.

Education does not exempt one from falling in the dark ranks of being a nigga. These educated niggas are definitely the ones you can't enlighten in any sense. Especially when suggesting that they look in the mirror. Having knowledge of different facts, dates, events, theories, equations, geographical locations, sciences, etc. has no bearing on the nature and behaviors of an individual, nor does that classify a person as intellectual. Educated or 'learned' is far more different than true intellect so let's not confuse the two. But when dealing with the black educated niggas, they have many theories as why the black race is in the current social, economical, and mental state it's in. And most times these learned and contemporary niggas point the blame to niggas, never realizing that they too are niggas. Just because the educated or successful nigga lives in a higher-class neighborhood and they associate themselves with a 'higher-class' of people, they assume that they are not and can never be a nigga. This is so far from the truth. Are these the ones that borrow the $20 dollars and not return the loan; probably not? But the situation doesn't necessarily have to be that of a loan for the chain of events; the before mentioned victim role, attack on your character, and controversy, to take place. It could've been that the nigga borrowed their neighbor's lawnmower, or a suitcase, whatever, and when asked to return the item, there starts the chain reaction. Also, does belonging to this higher-educated and/or higher-class stop the individuals from making excuses for all of their actions, or maybe always trying to hustle and manipulate their way through life on a daily basis, or stop them from being trifling? No it does not! These characteristics are the traits of a nigga. Again, a nigga can't be boxed into a specific race, educational background, or social class. A nigga can be found in any setting, having come from any background, and associate with any group of people. I'm willing to bet that a nigga has traveled into space. I say this to say that there is no running away from a nigga!

NO RUNNING AWAY FROM A NIGGA!!! NOWHERE TO RUN! I've learned that niggas are found everywhere and are present in every walk of life…from our neighborhoods, jobs, and families, even church! In the black society, we have labeled niggas as either a house nigga or a field slave. The house nigga being of course the one that obliges and bows to whatever the white man says. The house nigga is a poisonous serpent to his/her own race by definition of betrayal and disloyal to blacks; infiltrating the ranks of the field Negro, only to unveil any plans the field negro had of escaping and/or uprising to the white master. The field slave is completely opposite of the before mentioned. They are deemed to be loyal to their race. These two very different individuals were defined hundreds of years ago by African slaves and slave owners. But I do need to point out that there is a very distinct difference between a house slave and a house nigga…the difference being in the mentality.

A house nigga can no more be a house slave than a fox can be the hound, and likewise with the field slave versus the field nigga. For obvious reasons, the house negro was the black slave that was "allowed" to perform a lifetime of household servitudes for the slave master; i.e. cooking, cleaning, etc., and these house slaves were treated a bit better than their counterparts, the field slaves, who worked in the fields all day under the brutal and inhuman conditions and treatment of the slave overseers and owners. Make no mistake about it, the house slaves' duties were endless as well. The living conditions they 'stood' in were better than the field slave, but those conditions were made better by the fruits of their labor. Young house slaves, as early as five years of age, were bred to entertain their even younger, infant and adolescent white masters in the 'big house'. These young black house slaves were nothing more than toys for the white children. As the black youth entertained (as did the 'fool' for the king) their young masters, the older house slaves' calling was to pamper and nurture the white occupants' every beckoned call…everything from fetching a cool drink to fanning the sweat from their white brows, and even bathing them. And I dare not even start on the many horrific accounts of savage rape the white overseers, owners, and lustful white teens committed against the black female slaves. But I only mention these few examples to put things in some sort of perspective that life as a house slave wasn't peaches and crème. The house slaves were rationed leftover straps from the slave masters' dinner table whereas the field slave ate whatever they could muster. But when discussing the house niggas, they readily conformed to be a slave.

The terms slave and enslaved are two different working parts or functions in the English language, one a noun and the latter being a verb. Africans, taken as prisoners of war by other Africans, were enslaved. They were physically contained and worked more so as indentured servants to the capturers (to enslave). But to disconnect a person mentally from their heritage, culture, family, religion, life, etc., and that person is mentally reconditioned to the enslaver's forced upon life of hard labor, unimaginable living conditions, foreign religion, and culture through various methods of fear is only a few components of what makes the slave.

Even though most of the slaves, field or house, born and died under such conditions that were forced upon them, they continued to have faith, and they chanted and song their native tongues till the last days of their lives. Some would revolt, flee, and rebel, willing to face consequences of death than to totally conform to their oppressor's terms of a slave's life. But the house nigga's mentality was acceptable of their master's expectations. They accepted the conditions they lived in, constructed their own reality to believe those conditions were good (week-old molted biscuits and bread found in corners and underneath dusted furniture that they were 'allowed' to eat, pieces of meat thrown from the master's plate for them or the house pet to fetch, etc.). The house nigga no more wanted to be in the fields than the black field slave wanted to be in those fields or better yet be a slave, so they, the house nigga, tried to make their lives as pleasant or manageable as possible under the given conditions by reporting any actions and plans the field slaves and house slaves were involved in that would be frowned upon by the white slave master. The house nigga formed a strange kind of attachment to his brutal and ungodly slave master, and acquired a peculiar love for his master. This was betrayal on the house nigga's part towards the field slave. This betrayal could not be met with retaliation from the field slave in most instances because the house nigga was somewhat considered a favorite 'pet' to the white slave owners and therefore they were partially protected in this aspect.

These very noticeable differences in treatment between the two kinds of slaves formed resentment between them. In today's black society those two terms and mentalities still linger; the field slave and house nigga…not in social class status but in mentality. It is considered a very low title, one of no honor, in the black community to be relegated from a black man or woman to a house nigga. One would much more be excepting of titles such as thief, liar, or even drunk than to be considered a house nigga. But the term's definition has been twisted in the minds of a nigga!

For instance, in the work place you may have a situation where two people hold supervisory positions; one black supervisor and one of any other race. When these two supervisors interact with a group of black workers, there is a very disturbing and noticeable difference in the interactions. When the supervisor of a different race instructs a nigga to do a particular task or have to reprimand the nigga for whatever reason, that nigga take the interactions between them at face value and go about his/her way whistling as he works so to speak. Now, given the same situation but change the viable from a different race supervisor to a black supervisor, and the episode is viewed very differently by the nigga. I want to emphasize the person that I'm addressing is a black nigga, not black person, and make this distinction crystal clear, and that these niggas are embedded deep in our community.

Now, the nigga sees the black supervisor as a traitor to his race; a house nigga. The nigga can't believe that the black supervisor came at him in that way by simple asking him to do his job, or have the audacity to reprimand his. So again, we will witness an attack on the black supervisor's character, and the nigga will once again be a victim. The black supervisor is labeled a house nigga in the twisted mind of a nigga, but who indeed has the house nigga mentality? The nigga bows and succumbs to whatever that supervisor of another race asks of him/her with no hesitation whereas he/she challenges his/her own black brothers or sisters authority. And in the minds of the niggas, they can never see this injustice that they have committed and continue to commit against the black man and woman. In the minds of niggas, the injustice is on the part of the black supervisor.

I can recall a specific incident that opened my eyes some many years ago. I was a young jit around 19 years old in the United States Army. I was stationed permanent party at the Fort Sill, Ok field artillery division. This particular day my section had just made it back to the 'rear' (barracks/post) from being in the field all day, and standard protocol before we got to call it a day was to organize everything in the motor pool. This day it was extremely cold and raining. Each raindrop that hit my face and skin slightly stung as I rushed from the motor pool to my barracks. Well, my gunnery sergeant, a good-spirited young black man, had accompanied my roommate and I to our room for evening chatter…nothing out of the ordinary. After a few minutes of chopping it up, he asked me to go back to the motor pool and straighten up the connex. Of course, I interpreted the order as a request and met it with resistance. *"Come on, Serg! Why I gotta do it?"* I can clearly recall the mild-mannered sergeant looking to me and saying, *"Now, you see Hollins if Sergeant Blah Blah* (our white section chief) *instructed you to do this, you wouldn't' have said a word! You would've went and did it without a second thought."* I thought of what he said briefly then made my way to the motor pool. He attempted to stop me by stating I could complete the task after it stopped raining, but I continued on. He was right on his analysis of me. I didn't realize I had that type of mentality, so I walked in that cold pouring rain towards the motor pool because I wanted to show the gunner sergeant, my brother, the utmost respect. From that moment on, I've tried to be cognizant of my behaviors and interactions with all. I considered myself blessed to had been shown this foolish way of thinking, that I never knew existed in me, by this man. I was able to see something ugly in the mirror instead of trying to justify my actions and make excuses. I felt since he was a black man he should be "cool" with letting me get a pass on the duties that needed to be performed. I wanted to get over!

The warped sense of reality of the nigga extends to whatever facet of life they attempt to get over in. I'm not a nigga and never will be for the obvious reasons of me not making excuses for myself, and I was able to see the wrongs he pointed out. You see, a nigga lives to get over, and again doesn't see a thing wrong with anything he/she does.

But there is also the nigga mind set when it comes to the ones that are in power. You know the type that comes around their race of subordinates and converse and interact with them as though he/she is a fair and genuine person. They will even charade as a confidant to your personal issues and work concerns. But the moment his/her superior (supervisor of a different race) comes around, their demeanor and interaction changes with the subordinates from kind and friendly to dry, demanding, often times mean, and they begin giving orders and directives to the workers in a demeaning manner as if this is what they feel their supervisor expects of them if they want to maintain their hollow position with the company. That masked confidant will use all that was talked in private with the worker against the worker by telling his/her superior of the discussions held between the two, but of course leaving out whatever he/she had added in the discussion. Repeating the grips as if the worker is a troublemaker. This is so close to what white slave masters instilled in the cowardly and disloyal black slaves when they would have the before mentioned slaves oversee other slaves on the plantation by ordering them around, physically assaulting them, and whipping them. And to further humiliate and degrade the already broken slave, the black slave overseer would be heard calling his fellow brothers and sisters held in captivity 'nigga'! The pendulum definitely swings swift and equally crucial and deadly in both directions when addressing the minds of niggas in every facet of life.

When patronizing a black owned business, the nigga is always looking to barging down the already established prices of that black business. The black nigga wants what is considered a 'hook-up' or cheaper price. But when patronizing with anyone of a different race, the black nigga has no problem paying the price that is set by the owner even when this price is higher than the one he/she was expecting to pay, or higher than that of a black business owner.

And then you have the nigga business owner or employee. Again, we will notice a difference in the service a black person will receive as opposed to the services someone of another race will receive from the same black nigga worker or owner. It is truly astonishing and sad all together. On countless occasions, I've entered different businesses ranging from banks, grocery stores, insurance firms, car dealerships, to fast food, and I've noticed how the black nigga worker/service provider or owner would be very short-tempered, dry in attitude, and appeared irritated and too busy towards myself and other black people. But that same black nigga would provide a much warmer service to a person of a different race. They will go out of their way to ensure that customer's needs and wants are met. And the nigga does this without even realizing his/her different treatments in regards to his/her race versus that of another. This is the nigga's mentality and again, they see nothing wrong in these very different interactions on their part. They only see wrongs when that black owner, supervisor, worker, or customer asks them to do what is expected of all, and that is to be treated the same in all regard.

Then we have the niggas in church. I won't spend much time talking about the church niggas due to the fact they are so parallel to the other niggas discussed. But I will give you one very peculiar mind-set of the church nigga's way of thinking. The church nigga has not one problem telling another church goer or person they have come in acquaintance with that may be going through some hardships in their life that these hardships were brought about due to the person's wrongful ways of living, and that these hardships are nothing less than Godly karma. But when these same nigga's, church niggas, are faced with hardships of a similar nature they see these as trials and tests of faith from God. How can the same hardships be viewed so differently? Only a nigga can answer that because only a nigga lives in the demented mental realms of a nigga's mind.

As we all have witnessed, a nigga is a very hard individual to get along with and even harder to understand. A nigga will test the patience of Job! I don't know if one can ever kill a nigga's way of thinking or even alter it. As for me, I live to protect my mind from those ways of thinking like a noble knight protecting his beautiful princess from the fire-breathing dragon; my mind being the princess and the nigga's mentality being the dragon. You will find niggas reading this and actually take offense to the things I'm addressing. Their attitude being, *"Who the hell does he this he is?"*

Well, for all of those posing such a question, let me just tell you who I am not... a nigga! And this, I say to the black niggas, *I'm your color, but I ain't your kind.* Our ways of thinking are far from parallel, and not even on the same spectrum. I don't partake in the hate and envy you niggas revel in; the low ambitions, and deceitful ways towards everyone you encounter. We all have our faults! But to not want to better these faults after they have been revealed to you is beyond my comprehension. I pray daily asking God to reveal my wrongs to me and help me better myself each and every day. And guide me along a bright path He chooses me to journey. That along is a lifetime of work, and that along occupies me enough whereas I don't have the time to focus on anything that is not beneficial, unlike you niggas.

The Production and Manufacturing of A Nigga

With all that's said surrounding what the nigga so readily imposes on society and their effects on society, let us briefly examine the production and manufacturing of these so-called niggas. And again, when analyzing such, it begins and ends with their peculiar state of mind. First, consider the possibility of them having not a clue as to what is really going on around them on a grander scale whether it be the poor and destitute niggas or the affluent ones. Plans that have been put into motion by the powers that be (the system/the elite), are designed for and survive off of clueless, uncaring, and nonchalant minds. Take for instance, the nigga recipients of government assistance. I stress nigga recipient, because there are so many misfortunate individuals that receive the same assistance due to disabilities or as a means to make ends meet until they can see a brighter day. The latter has no intentions of becoming dependents on such programs because they have plans to compete in today's work force.

Unfortunately, the physically and mentally disabled are limited in different areas, so these types of government programs are somewhat beneficial to them. (I do want to add that the sum allotted to the truly needy could not be measured in a fraction of a fraction as to what is required and deserved, and especially when referencing people of color due to all that was taken from African Americans and the Natives, the original occupants of this country. But again, that is another topic.) On any account, you have so many able-body niggas, both young and middle-aged, walking about daily that has been provided with such benefits. They proudly display these EBT cards and such as if they have no shame or a clue to the bigger picture and plan they have succumb to. And they have not one intention on finding work or pursuing a higher education to better themselves or better the lives of the many children they have so thoughtlessly brought into this cold world. The bigger picture is a conspiracy on the less fortunate; mainly people of color. These types of programs are developed by the 'elite' to be used as a permanent crippler instead of a temporary crutch to said people. These $500 to whatever monthly amount of fixed government income or stipends they receive, are kibbles compared to the $20 and $30k the givers take home each month. But niggas become complacent and satisfied with these crumbs. And once complacent, they have no intentions of doing better for themselves or their families by filling the work place or pursuing a higher education, and now they are no longer a threat to the 'system'. I say threat because if they are not trying to educate themselves and aggressively awake on a conscious level to become peers to the powers that be, by putting themselves in the same if not higher positions, then they pose no significant threat at all to these 'powers'. This becomes a cycle that is rarely broken in the life of niggas.

I once heard that most people walk a circle their entire life that appears to be a straight line. This was so abstruse to me. People walking until their demise, assuming they are moving forward in an effort to advance in life but never realizing that what appears as a 'straight line' to them is nothing more than a circle. This mental circle keeps the blind enveloped and limited to so much in life, mainly progress on many levels. How profound. This definitely applies to the nigga. They have no earthly idea as to what the bigger picture is; equivalent to not being able to see the forest for the trees. So, in not being able to see this broad circle that appears to be a straight line, the nigga passes these blind lifestyles down to their children, and their children's children. We all, as children, often model our surroundings, and rarely is that cycle broken. So in mimicking this perception, the children will grow and live out their adult lives traveling in a circle and never progressing. This is but one way to produce a nigga environment, and by keeping this cycle going, the 'system' manufactures countless niggas daily.

The high-end nigga hasn't a clue to these conspiracies either. They assume they are 'in' with the powers that be when the elite grant them morsels of power over things of little to no importance. This also keeps these high-end niggas occupied and their attention diverted. This is also reproduced in their children. This continuation is the results of nigga parents passing down their knowledge, views, and perception on life to their children: all, which are tainted and warped.

Nigga parenting is when two niggas of the opposite sex decide to commit with each other in sexual reproduction. The result is an innocent lost! What possibly could the corrupted minds of these individuals pass off to this infant child? A child being raised by two nigga parents is all but hopeless. What more can be said for such a situation? This poor child's mind will be nurtured by the 'clueless'. What can the 'unknowing' teach a young and starving mind? How can a 'seasoned blind' lead such an innocent blind? As sad as the situation sounds, such situation does exist, and on a grand scale. Here we have yet another facet in the production and manufacturing of the nigga. And only Divine interventions can help such a child.

We also have what's being programed in our minds daily by the media; from the televised shows and music channels we watch to what's heard on the news and radio stations. They create an image of who's who, what's to be sought after, what's cool, what's right and wrong, and so forth. And we often make mental agreements on a conscious level with these things. But what if you wake mentally one day and redefine what is happiness, failure, success, love, strength, weakness, etc., to you and apply these things in your life: reconditioning your mind? The 'system' will be useless, a failure... become obsolete. Compare what I'm asking to the multi-million dollar movie 'The Matrix'! Which pill will you take after being awakened to such social injustices? My cousin often says to me that if you change your way of thinking then you change your reality. I totally agree. You might not be able to change your surroundings but you can change how your surroundings affect you and the ways you interact with these surroundings. Most won't wake, and I'm not just referring to the niggas, but even being exposed to truths, a nigga will still take the pill the 'system' has been prescribing to them their entire life. And for these types of foolish individuals, the ones that are awake need to change how they interact with them, if at all, and view these as lost and clueless niggas. Remember what they say, "*I might can't stop you from shitting, but I can damn sho slow you down!*" You can't change their ways of thinking, but you definitely don't have to contribute to the system or these niggas fool-ways. A nigga's facade of reality is that of a dark and twisted state of living. The conditioning of a mind cannot be underestimated by anyone. Let's not sleep with or beside the niggas! Let's be cognizant of the system as a whole and wake to redefine ourselves in a pure light; not what was and is fed to us. And in redefining ourselves, we can redefine our surroundings.

The Disconnect

My earlier brief addressing, of a slave versus being enslaved, intent was to focus on a mind state. I've heard that black people's greatest moments of pride were the '60s. I don't know, and I won't try and argue that. We had countless obstacles, factors, and government agencies working against us since we as a people were kidnapped and shipped in chains to this country. Life for blacks in America has never been and could never be fully captured in words, dialog, film, or pictures. From the depriving of basic human rights, barbaric living conditions, starvation, humiliation and cruelties of having to survive off flour, corn and water all mixed and matted together and called daily meals, uncooked pig fats eaten and used as remedies and medical treatments, slave hands preparing festive meals only to watch and smell the sweet simmering meats and bakeries being eaten by their masters, unbearable stenches from living beside and sometimes with the field animals and poorly kept livestock, living in and around human waist, births delivered by overworked field hands in pig-sties and on loosely rotted-wooden floors, unrelenting toils- backbreaking work loads and work days till their death, aches and pains from bruised and broken bones that went unattended due to their daily forced free labor, open wounds left to drip-dry of blood, backs terribly beaten with treated leather and the lash marks and cuts cared for by pouring red peppers and salts in and over the wounds, the inhuman psych of the oppressors, rape, heartache, male pride and protection of his woman being dissipated to terror stricken, lamblike behaviors and attitudes and total obedience to their master, beatings, killings, swaying dead bodies (often burned, elevated to a height to be publicized, made example of and boasted about), torn and ripped flesh, amputated limbs, dug-out eyeballs, bashed in skulls, castrations, mutilations, bodies riddled with bullets, torn families through relocation by means of selling, literally blistering heats or frost bitten days and night to work and sleep in, no voice on hostel soils, etc., day in and out till the point the victims and the violators become numb to it all can never be fully appreciated unless one lived it. I can be much more long-winded, and descriptive of the knowledge I've obtained about slave life, and not one could argue or categorize my endless pen on such matters as being verbose…but why go on? What can I, or anyone for that matter, possibly say that can accurately describe what our people went through, their hardships, trial, tribulations, the atrocities readily placed upon them? I, for one, could never internalize such feelings- **the life of a slave**.

Then we are emancipated, so-called set free…only to face the same and often times, harsher conditions in the antebellum South and all across the states under new well thought-out plans to restrict blacks. But it was the same game with the same players, only with different terminology and legislation such as segregation, share croppers, vagrancy laws, the black codes, anti-miscegenation laws, disenfranchisement, denying blacks suffrage through the grandfather clauses of the South, low wages, debt, and discriminations on every level, which influenced the Jim Crow laws which in turn produced a movement on our part to demand, instead of seeking and asking, for our rights, and respect.

Along came countless black leaders and prophets in the form of Booker T. Washington, Malcolm X, Dr. Martin Luther King, Stokey Carmichael, Marcus Garvey, Huey P. Newton, Angela Davis, twenty-one year old Fred Hampton, Bobby Seale, and so many other dignified and educated brothers and sisters which were targeted by racist individuals, organizations, mobs, clans, black nigga informants which were tossed kibbles in monetary compensation, police, local and state governments, and even worse, federal government agencies led by the J. Hoovers of the time in most of these corrupt clandestine activities. These attacks by said groups were orchestrated and carried out under unlawful and illegal means to keep us down economically, socially, culturally, spiritually, and mentally. The CoIntelPro was developed just to study, infiltrate, and destroy our unity…billions and billions of dollars spent on such tasks. Their politically correct reasoning was/is to maintain the social order (i.e., status in quo) of this great nation…the task truly being to disconnect us as a people from our history and ourselves.

What we have to examine and understand are the links and ties of these programs, idealisms, policies, agencies, and so forth, which were and still are committing such atrocities to our people. Who were/are they, and why target the Black race? After slavery was so-call abolished, the four million Blacks in America were somewhat useless to the economy. Fact being, many with 'real wealth' seen our race as now being a liability to the nation's economy whereas, before the emancipation doctrine, black slaves were an asset. The white 'elite' labeled this a serious problem. The millions of Whites in the country only seen and still see the small picture just as the American black man and woman. What the common white person thought to be a problem when referencing the newly freed slaves was their uselessness in the work force if they couldn't be kept in the fields to plant, grow, and harvest their cotton, rice, sugar, and tobacco products. So, this group of people came up with brilliant ways to keep Blacks enslaved legally without it being called slavery- the black codes. These ideals were carefully though out and carried out during the Reconstruction Period. But the elite Whites deemed us as a treat to their race. Here so came the ideals to colonize the newly freed blacks by sending them back to Africa. They couldn't dare risk the chance of interracial relations that would destroy such a pure and Divine-entitled white race. This particular idea was short lived due to radical thinkers on the local and political fronts. So came the in-depth practice of eugenics (or race hygiene as called by the Germans) founded by Francis Galton, cousin to James Darwin. American Eugenicists believed there is an elite race, and there is a feebleminded, docile, and worthless race of people-…we fell/fall under the latter in their analysis. American

Eugenicists published countless papers and books, and performed just as many studies on these ideals, then poured their spotted and polluted thinking onto an already bitter white nation that resented Blacks. The conclusion by their consensus was/is the black population need be exterminated, but it would be unlawful under the newly adopted amendments making us legal citizens so they devise (d) plans to sterilize our race. Here lies one tie we must recognize with the American Birth Control League, (presently called Planned Parenthood) founded by Margaret Sanger, and the American Eugenics Society.

They called for the sterilization of the black race by any means necessary including involuntary sterilizations, which they performed. Sanger was quoted as saying, "*I believe that the world and almost all civilization ...is going to depend upon a simple, cheap, safe contraceptive to be used in poverty stricken slums, jungles, and among the most ignorant people. Even this will not be sufficient, because I believe that now, immediately, there should be national sterilization for certain dysgenic types of our population who are being encouraged to breed and would die out were the government not feeding them.*" They believed that the only way to downsize or depopulate the black race was through controlled fertilization. These ideals and practices were so well received that Adolf Hitler recognized, praised, and reached out to the Eugenicists in America. He adopted their philosophies and executed them in what is known as the Holocaust. Now, we are aware of their plan. What we see are the faces in our every day life, but have we defined these faces and their roles in our every day life?

Here's some food for thought, studies show that majority of the women that require hysterectomies are of African decent. An astonishing 65.4% of the cases associated with uterine fibroids leading to a hysterectomy were black females. Uterine fibroids are noncancerous tumors that develop in the womb. Causes for this growth are unknown. *In a study of more than 53,000 hysterectomies, black women were more than twice as likely to have a diagnosis of uterine fibroids as white women*[1]... We all know what a hysterectomy is. My question is why are the choices reduced largely in favor to this procedure? Why is our female race so susceptible to the growth of fibroids on their reproductive organs? I discussed such matters with a dear friend of mine, and we theorized the following. The everyday doctors you and I frequent are not the researchers, they are not the ones dressed in white lab jackets. They only practice a health care that they have been taught, but taught by who…the researchers. So their prognosis for any medical treatment needed is indeed predetermined…but again, by whom? And what are the other choices our black sisters have other than a hysterectomy? Our 'visible' black and white doctors do serve as vital instruments and often times heroes to the general population, but we must consider that they are no more in the light on certain situations than we as patients are, especially when it comes to top secret tests and research (recalling accounts of the Tuskegee experiments) for the better and survival of the current status in quo, being the 'elite'. These doctors, surgeons, etc. are only delivering to us a service they are trained and programmed to deliver, as are political and religious leaders. I won't go into extensive detail of the Eugenicists practices. My goal is to only introduce to you an overall plan on the part of the elite.

---

[1] PMID 8414322(PubMed –indexed for MEDLINE)

I am driven to believe that we must really be some kind of a special race for the 'elite' to take notice of and try to embed a global dissonance upon us! I consciously scribed a lower case 'e' when identifying with the elite to show my lack of respect for them. My focus is on the Elite Black race and any race calling for harmony between the races. So with the before mentioned knowledge, begin to ask yourselves, who are 'we'? Were we truly kings and queens in a time? Did Egypt belong to us? Were the pyramids and such great wonders of the world, built with our minds? Did we study the stars and planets? Did we create and solve complex mathematical equations? Did we nurture a part of history they have attempted to erase? Were we a bold, noble, and regal people of royalty and wealth? Who exactly are we? What is a race of people that has been disconnected from their heritage and knowledge of self?

We are the chosen! But we, as a whole, do not share my views of being a special people. Many of you have been conditioned by the oppressors to remain oppressed. You are slaves. You have been disconnected from who we are as a people. Our location here in America or any other part of this small planet is of little to no importance if we don't know how we are. They have printed, taught, campaigned, and preached throughout the years that we are a worthless, lazy, carefree, stupid, and a docile race of people. And through this repetitive propaganda, both conscious and subconscious, many of you have made a mental agreement with them to live up to these ways. And even in saying this, if we are all what white racist America along with its elite say we are, we still can not hold a candle to all the negative, evil, demonic, and twisted attributes which define their conscious, spiritual, and moral make-up. They are a people of parasitic nature who unleashed atrocities on every person of color.

Yes, in many ways I argue with the system on its self-imposed description of black people. We are a beautiful race! We are inventors, artists, doctors, scientists, philosophers, poets, space travelers, noble mothers and fathers, proud sons and daughters, presidents, great husbands and wives, teachers, spiritual deliverers, actors, ballerinas, gold-metal Olympians, hard-workers, professional businessmen and women, professional athletes, attempters, doers, dreamers, victors, survivors, etc. But even when addressing the black 'nigga', I have but this to argue with the powers that be. They (other races and some of us in the black race) accuse the nigga as being lazy, but I beg to differ. A nigga works extremely hard, day in and out, to make sure they have absolutely nothing of substance in life. They do not strive to obtain things that can benefit them in life as fine homes, happiness, love, credit, money, family, pride, their history, their future, a future for the children they bring into this world, etc., so they work each day to either destroy or put as much distance possible between these things and themselves. That's a hard, unrelenting work ethic if I've never seen one.

Muddy Wings

Can the rage manifested inside propel me to a soaring flight, I often wonder
Fly away lost soul! Fly away!
There's a fire inside of me that electrifies
Breaking the ties of my consciousness and soul
I tossed that connect somewhere along the dirt road he swings from
Pine straw, oak- and so nearby pokes ol magnolia
So say Mother Earth, "Your worth is the dirts he bleeds upon."
Fly away!
"A storm's ah cummin!" Old worked hands with dull brown/yellow cataract eyes that's
not permitted to cry would say...in pain and struggle song
Rags religiously worn that hangs with sun-blackened skin
He grins as I grin. His smile stretches over loose teeth
I stare off into a summer night breeze and dream to
Fly away!
But my black wings are often weighed with the hard Mississippi clays
I sit tireless in my greys
Cause today that ol storm resides inside of me
LSohl

Connecting

I seriously doubt if we can change a nigga! But in saying this, I also want to stress that if we wake mentally and look in our 'mirror', we will see so much work that needs to be done in our lives. This work will take so much time and energy that I'm all but certain none of us will even possess the time to try and change a nigga. So start with self! Work on self by redefining the truths and agreements you have made with society…redefine these to suit your life. While working on self, you will be affecting family and close friends, and hungry minds and spirits will absorb this positivity. The family structure is of utter most importance. This can't be stressed enough. We have to first discipline our minds, emotions, and spirits to the task of reconditioning. Then and only then can we disciple our children by teaching them what has been revealed to us, and embedding these positives into their lives so they too can pass them on to their children when that time comes.

We, as responsible adults and parents have to get involved with the school systems because a child is going to be just that, a child. In us acknowledging this, we know kids will and they are going to test the waters to see what they can and cannot get away with. And if the teachers and school system does not have the backing of the parents, our kids will attend with minimal awareness dedicated to their classes, they will act out time and time again knowing there is no consequence waiting for them at home. They will be disrespectful to their teachers, authority figures, and to their peers. They will not strive to reach their potential if we as parents have not put forth an effort to reach ours. We must be their role models! We must become as much of a 'hero' as we can be to them. All of these things start at home. All of these things start with self! So by us awakening, and reconditioning ourselves, then facilitating and teaching our families, we in turn break the circle that appeared as a straight line.

I feel one of the most resourceful institutions that is at our disposal is the church. Here gathers our communities. The church embodies people from all different backgrounds, collectively possessing every skill one can imagine. I say to the many churches that only open their doors on Sunday, try everyday. At any given church, its congregation is composed of teachers, lawyers, doctors, nurses, therapists, agriculturalists, environmentalists, mechanics, pilots, bankers, small business owners, a multitude of professionals, mothers, fathers, big brothers and sisters, etc. The church officials should reach out to these members of good faith, and ask them to schedule a portion of their free time throughout the week where they can devise and incorporate programs to educate the young and old. Bankers, teach them the importance of saving money and how to budget. Teachers, help the children in areas they struggle academically, or the adult that wants to further his/her education. Nurses and doctors, talk to our teens about safe sex. Talk to families about ailments they might be facing. Small business owners, help the aspiring entrepreneur devise a business plan as you have. And many people are only in need of a listening ear, not wanting to be judged, but just someone to listen to them. Open the doors to the church not only on Sunday but everyday and help with the healing of our communities.

These daily programs require no money…only time. And if each one teaches one, we will, in turn, change a lot about our surroundings, then this nigga population will become so minute and of the minority that if we stay consistent, their ways, nor the plans of the 'system' and elite, will have much effect on our society. We shall be free by ridding ourselves of such belittling philosophies, practices, and its institutions of self-hate that cling onto so much of our race! We will reconnect with our noble ancestors and our royal past. And by doing these things, we will propagate the true face of the African American race. We will awaken and break the mental chains that currently enslave us! Only then will we truly be free.

"Were even paradise itself my prison,
       still I should long to leap the crystal walls."
       John Dryden: Poet/Playwright/Critic

Timothy Hollins/LSohl: Author/Poet/Spoken Work
Literary Muse Publications
Trhollins@aol.com
(404) 432-2993
Twitter @LSohl1

www.ingramcontent.com/pod-product-compliance
Lightning Source LLC
Chambersburg PA
CBHW070838310526
45788CB00017B/2082